Squirrel R

for the

Zombie Apocalypse

Introduction

In these troubling times, the end of days may be near. If the zombie apocalypse happens, those that survive may need to make due with wild game for food. Squirrels are resourceful animals and are prolific breeders. They are likely to survive the zombie apocalypse. If your stock piles of food have been depleted or if you were not a good doomsday prepper and have not adequately prepared for the zombie apocalypse, you may need to make some concessions to feed your family or yourself.

Squirrel meat will be plentiful, so it just stands to reason that cooking squirrels may be necessary for your survival. Don't worry, when adequately prepared, squirrel can be quite tasty and is currently enjoyed by many people in remote locations such as the Ozark Mountains or by lost hikers and campers.

Keep this cookbook whenever you are camping, prepping or boondocking so that you can easily prepare your freshly caught squirrel. This cookbook is full of delicious and tasty squirrel recipes to help the survivalist, not only survive but to thrive through the zombie apocalypse.

How to Field Dress a Squirrel

This method helps to preserve the hide in case it is needed to make clothing or bedding in the zombie apocalypse.

1. Using game shears or a sharp knife, make a cut on the belly, making sure not to cut too deep. In other words, just cut the hide, not the meat.
2. Cut all the way around the torso just under the skin. Work your fingers under the skin and pull in the opposite direction. Snip the legs, neck and tail off.
3. Cut at the joints, right above the feet and at the base of the tail.
4. Cut through the neck and remove the head.
5. Insert the knife or shears in the anus and make a cut through the pelvis up to the neck.
6. Using two fingers, grab the heart, lungs and esophagus and pull the innards towards the tail. This should remove all the innards, including the intestines to end up with a clean internal cavity.
7. Use water to give it a quick rinse and put it in a zip lock bag if you are taking it home. Soak the squirrel in a salty brine overnight to draw out more of the blood.
8. Remember to always thoroughly cook your squirrel in order to prevent any diseases, such as rabies.

Beer Basted Rabbit

Ingredients:

3 pounds squirrel meat
2 tbsps. garlic salt
2 (12 fluid oz.) cans beer

Directions:

1. Preheat grill to medium high and lightly oil grate.
2. Place squirrel meat on heated grill and season with garlic salt.
3. Pour beer into a medium bowl.
4. Let meat cook 15 minutes, then start basting with beer every 10 minutes until done, about 30 minutes.

Squirrel Curry

Ingredients:

1/4 cup ghee (clarified butter), or vegetable oil
2 pounds hare or squirrel meat, cut off the bone and into chunks
Salt
2 cups yellow or white onion, sliced root to tip
2 tbsps. minced ginger
2 tbsps. minced garlic
A 14-oz. can of tomato puree
1 cup Greek plain yogurt
2 cups water
2 bay leaves
1 heaping tsp. turmeric
1/4 cup curry paste, or 2 tbsps. curry powder
1 tbsp. garam masala
1/4 cup chopped cilantro for garnish

Directions:

1. Heat the clarified butter in a wide pot (like a sauce pot or high-sided frying pan with a lid) over medium-high heat. Pat the hare pieces dry with paper towels and brown them well. Salt the meat as it cooks.
2. Remove to a bowl once browned.
3. Add the onion and saute until it begins to brown at the edges, about 5 minutes.
4. Add the ginger and garlic and cook another minute.
5. Return the meat to the pot and add the tomato puree, water, bay leaves, turmeric and Madras curry paste.
6. Stir in the yogurt and bring to a gentle simmer.
7. Add salt to taste and simmer for 30 minutes.
8. Finish by stirring in the Garam Masala and the cilantro. Serve over rice.

Squirrel Fricassee

Ingredients:

2 cups red wine
2 tbs. lemon juice
2 bay leaves
1 tsp. thyme
¼ tsp. marjoram
1 tsp. garlic powder
2 squirrels, cutin to pieces
2 tbs. olive oil
1 onion, chopped
2 garlic, minced
2 tbs. cornstarch
Salt and Pepper to taste

Directions:

1. Mix wine, lemon juice, bay leaves, thyme, marjoram, salt, pepper and garlic powder to make marinade.
2. Place squirrel in large bowl and pour marinade over squirrel.
3. Cover and refrigerate overnight.
4. Remove squirrel from marinade when ready to cook and pat dry.
5. Strain marinade and save.
6. Heat oil in a large skillet.
7. Sauté onions and garlic, add squirrel pieces and pour marinade over the top, cover and simmer 1 - 1 ½ hours or until tender.

Buttermilk Fried Squirrel

Ingredients:

2 to 4 cottontails, cut into serving pieces
2 cups buttermilk
2 tbsps. Italian seasoning
1 tbsp. paprika
1 tbsp. garlic powder
2 tsps. cayenne, or to taste
1 1/2 cups flour
1 heaping tsp. salt
About 2 cups vegetable oil

Directions:

1. Mix the buttermilk with the all the spices except the tsp. of salt and the flour.
2. Coat the squirrel with the mixture and set in a covered container overnight, or at least 8 hours.
3. When you are ready to fry, pour the oil into a large pan — a big cast iron frying pan is ideal — to a depth of about an inch.
4. The general idea is you want the oil to come halfway up the side of the squirrel. Set the heat to medium-high.
5. Meanwhile, take the squirrel out of the buttermilk and let it drain in a colander. Don't shake off the buttermilk or anything, just leave it there.
6. Let the oil heat until it is about 325 degrees F; this is the point where a sprinkle of flour will immediately sizzle.
7. When the oil is hot, pour the flour and salt into a plastic bag and shake to combine.
8. Put a few pieces of squirrel into the bag and shake to get it coated in flour.
9. Set the coated squirrel pieces in one layer in the hot oil so they don't touch.
10. Fry for about 8 to 12 minutes.
11. Turn the squirrel pieces and fry for another 10 minutes or so, until they are golden brown.

12. When the squirrel is good and fried, let them rest on a rack set over a paper towel to drain away any excess oil.
13. If you are cooking in batches, set this in a warm oven.

Greek Squirrel

Ingredients:

1/4 cup olive oil
1 (3 pound) squirrel, cut into pieces
2 bay leaves
1 tsp. salt
4 whole allspice berries
1/2 tsp. oregano
1 lemon, juiced
1/2 cup white wine
warm water, to cover

Directions:

1. Heat 1/4 cup olive oil in a large saucepan over medium heat. Fry squirrel pieces in hot oil until evenly browned.
2. Season with bay leaves, salt, allspice berries, oregano, and lemon juice to the saucepan.
3. Pour white wine over the squirrel.
4. Bring the mixture to a simmer; cook 4 to 5 minutes.
5. Add enough water to the saucepan to cover squirrel completely.
6. Bring the liquid to a simmer.
7. Cook until squirrel is cooked through and the water is evaporated, about 40 minutes.

Spanish Squirrel

Ingredients:

2 whole squirrels
4 cloves garlic, finely chopped
2 onions, sliced
1 can (16 oz.) crushed tomatoes
1 bay leaf
1 sprig tarragon
1 sprig thyme
2 stalks celery, finely chopped
1 cup white wine
1/2 cup water
salt and pepper to taste
1 sprig parsley
extra virgin olive oil

Directions:

1. Clean the squirrel, if necessary.
2. Cut squirrel in small pieces (approximately 12-15 pieces).
3. Chop onions, garlic and celery.
4. Pour enough olive oil into the bottom of large, heavy frying pan and heat on medium high. When hot enough, place squirrel in pan and brown the pieces on all sides.
5. Remove and set aside.
6. Using the same pan, sauté the garlic, onion and crushed tomatoes for about 5 minutes. (If ingredients begin to stick, add more olive oil if necessary.)
7. Add the bay leaf, tarragon, thyme and chopped celery.
8. Return the squirrel to the frying pan.
9. Add the white wine and stir. Turn the heat up to bring to a boil and reduce the liquid by a half or two-thirds.
10. Then, add the water and stir.
11. Reduce heat.

12. Cover the pan and simmer gently until cooked – an hour and a half to two hours. (If using chicken instead of squirrel, it will take only 30-45 minutes.)
13. While the meat is simmering, chop parsley.
14. Adjust salt and pepper.
15. Sprinkle with chopped parsley and serve hot in bowls with fried potatoes and rustic bread.

Belgian Squirrel

Ingredients:

3 larges squirrels, skinned and gutted
1/2 cup butter
2 onions, sliced
On Sale
3 tbsps. white vinegar
1/8 tsp. dried thyme
salt and pepper to taste
18 pitted prunes
1 1/2 tsps. all-purpose flour
1 cup cold water

Directions:

1. Clean squirrels, making sure that all shot is removed. Burn away with a candle any fur that clings.
2. Rinse the meat though several changes of water and pat dry.
3. Cut squirrels into serving pieces.
4. Preheat the oven to 350 degrees F (175 degrees C).
5. Melt the butter in a large skillet over medium heat.
6. Add squirrel pieces and fry until browned on all sides, but do not cook through.
7. Remove the squirrel pieces to a large Dutch oven or oven safe crock.
8. Add onions to the butter in the skillet; cook and stir until tender and browned.
9. Pour the onions and butter into the pot with the squirrel.
10. Fill with enough water to almost cover the meat.
11. Mix in the vinegar and season with thyme, salt and pepper.
12. Cover and place in the oven.
13. Bake for 1 hour in the preheated oven.
14. Remove the pot from the oven and add the prunes. Return to the oven and reduce the heat to 325 degrees F (165 degrees C). Continue baking for another 45 minutes.
15. Remove the pot from the oven.
16. Mix the flour and cold water together in a cup.

17. Use a slotted spoon to remove the meat and prunes to a serving dish. Set the pot on the stove and bring to a boil over medium-high heat.
18. Stir in the flour and water and simmer, stirring constantly, until the gravy is thick enough to coat a metal spoon.
19. Serve meat with a lot of gravy.

Squirrel Legs

Ingredients:

8 oz. sliced bacon
16 meaty squirrel legs
Salt and pepper, to taste
1/2 cup all-purpose flour
1/2 cup cornstarch
2 eggs
2 tbsps. milk
1 cup thinly sliced onions
2 tbsps. minced garlic
2 tbsps. minced shallot
1 cup chicken stock1 bay leaf
1 tsp. minced fresh thyme

Directions:

1. Cook the bacon in a large skillet over medium heat until crispy; drain on paper towels, cool and crumble; set aside.
2. Reserve grease in the skillet.
3. While the bacon is cooking, season the squirrel with salt and pepper, and set aside.
4. In a resealable bag, mix together flour and cornstarch. Whisk together eggs and milk until smooth. Dredge the squirrel in the flour mixture, shake off excess flour, then dip into egg mixture, shaking off excess egg. Dredge again in the flour, and set aside.
5. Pour all but two tbsps. of bacon fat from the skillet, and place over medium-high heat. When the fat is hot, cook the squirrel pieces until golden brown, 3 to 4 minutes per side, then set aside.
6. Turn heat down to medium; add the onions, garlic, and shallot and cook for 3 minutes, until soft.
7. Pour in the chicken stock, and add the bay leaf and minced thyme. Increase heat to medium-high and bring to a simmer.
8. Add the squirrel, return to a simmer, cover, then turn heat to medium-low.
9. Cook until very tender, about 30 minutes.

10. Remove the squirrel legs to a serving platter and spoon the sauce over them.
11. Sprinkle with crumbled bacon and serve.

Slow Cooker Squirrel and Liver

Ingredients:

1 tbsp. olive oil
2 squirrels, skinned, gutted, and cut into pieces
2 lbs. beef liver, sliced into thin strips
2 large sweet onions, chopped
4 carrots, sliced
1 green bell pepper, seeded and sliced into strips
6 cloves garlic, minced
2 cups tomato juice
1 tsp. salt
1 tsp. ground black pepper
1 tsp. dried oregano
1 tsp. crushed dried thyme
1 bay leaf

Directions:

1. Heat the olive oil in a large skillet over medium heat. Sear the squirrel and liver until browned on the outside. Transfer to a slow cooker.
2. Add the onions, carrots, bell pepper and garlic.
3. Stir in the tomato juice.
4. Season with salt, pepper, oregano, thyme and bay leaf.
5. Cover, and cook on High for 6 hours.

Slow Cooker Squirrel and Veggies

Ingredients:

1 onion, cut into chunks
2 cups baby carrots
4 large potatoes, cut into small chunks
1 large green bell pepper, cut into chunks
2 cloves garlic4 cubes chicken bouillon
Salt and pepper to taste
3 squirrels, skinned, gutted, and cut into pieceswater to cover
2 tbsps. flour

Directions:

1. Place the onion, carrots, potatoes, bell pepper, garlic, chicken bouillon, salt, and pepper in a slow cooker.
2. Lay the squirrel meat on top of the vegetable mixture.
3. Pour enough water over the mixture to cover completely.
4. Cover and cook on HIGH 6 hours.
5. Stir the flour into the mixture and cook another 2 hours.

Slow Cooked Squirrel

Ingredients:

2 squirrels, skinned, gutted, and cut into pieces
4 large potatoes, quartered
1 lb. carrots, chopped
1 green bell pepper, chopped
4 onions, sliced
2 cups water
1/4 medium head cabbage
1 tsp. salt
1 tsp. ground black pepper

Directions:

1. In a slow cooker, place the squirrel meat, potatoes, carrots, green bell pepper, onions, water, cabbage, salt and ground black pepper.
2. Cover and cook on low setting for 8 hours.

Baked Squirrel

Ingredients:

4 cut up squirrels (use only hind legs and meaty back pieces)
1 chopped green sweet pepper
1/4 cube butter
4 tbsp. red cooking wine
1 can cream of mushroom soup
1/4 cup vinegar
1 lg. chopped onion
4 tbsp. salt
1 tsp. Adolph's tenderizer
2 tsp. pepper
1 cup flour
Crisco and cooking oil

Directions:

1. Mix vinegar and salt with water to cover squirrel. Soak 2 hours in solution.
2. Remove pieces and shake on tenderizer and pepper.
3. Roll in flour.
4. Fry in Crisco until brown.
5. Place pieces in baking dish.
6. In another skillet saute onion and pepper in butter.
7. Add wine and soup.
8. Mix well.
9. Pour over squirrel.
10. Bake at 300 degrees for 45 minutes.

Broiled Squirrel

Ingredients:

2 squirrels
1 tsp. salt
1/4 tsp. pepper
4 tbsp. melted bacon fat

Directions:

1. Skin and clean the squirrels.
2. Wash and pat dry.
3. Cut in half lengthwise and remove the head.
4. Rub the squirrels with salt and pepper.
5. If in camp, place the halved squirrels on a broiling rack and brush with the bacon fat.
6. Broil 8 inches away from heat for 30 minutes.
7. Baste every 5 minutes with bacon fat. If on the trail, spear the whole squirrel on a stick and put it in front of the camp fire, basting and turning the stick occasionally for at least 45 minutes.
8. A few apples on a stick propped in front of the fire will complement this dish very well.

Country Style squirrel

Ingredients:

2 squirrels
Salt & pepper to taste
Flour
6 tbsp. vegetable oil
2 cup water

Directions:

1. Cut squirrel into small chunks of frying size pieces, salt and pepper then roll in flour until coated well.
2. Put in skillet of hot oil and fry until golden.
3. Remove squirrel and most the oil, then add water and bring to boil.
4. Place squirrel back into the skillet, turn to low heat, cover and cook for approximately 1 hour.
5. Serve with some large potatoes that have been baked for a great combination.

Oven-Fried Squirrel

Ingredients:

1 squirrel
4 eggs
bread crumbs
Flour
Olive oil
Canola oil/ vegetable oil
Butter

Directions:

1. Pat meat dry with paper towel to remove any moisture.
2. Dip squirrel in egg.
3. Combine bread crumbs with flour, dip egg-covered squirrel in mix.
4. Cover bottom of skillet with olive oil and canola oil, add butter and brown meat well (about 20 min). Put squirrel in baking dish and pour contents of skillet over meat.
5. Bake for one hour at 375 degrees F.

Squirrel Country Sausage

Ingredients:

4 1/2 lbs. squirrel (approx. 15 fox squirrels)
1 Tbsp. sage
2 lbs. fresh seasoned pork sausage (with sage)
2 tsp. basil
1 onion
3 tsp. margarine
3 garlic cloves
1 tbsp. chili powder
4 tbsp. fresh parsley
1 tbsp. black pepper
2 tbsp. salt
1 tsp. thyme

Directions:

1. De-bone the squirrel and chop in food processor.
2. Mix together with fresh pork. Mince the onion and garlic (Use a tbsp. of garlic powder if you don't have cloves).
3. Cook the onion until transparent and add the garlic and sauté slightly.
4. Mix together meats, onion, garlic and herbs.
5. To test seasonings, form a small patty and fry in a cast iron frying pan with butter. Taste and adjust seasonings accordingly.
6. Form into small patties to cook or grill and use with your favorite sausage recipes.

Broccoli Squirrel Casserole

Ingredients:

6 squirrels
1 bag frozen broccoli pieces
1 lg. onion
4 carrots
Bread crumbs
1 (8 oz.) pkg. sharp cheddar cheese
8 oz. light cream
1 cup butter
Basil to taste
1 tsp. lemon juice

Directions:

1. Skin clean and quarter squirrels.
2. Boil in large pot with water and chicken bouillon cube until tender.
3. Set aside until cool and then bone completely until only meat remains.
4. Microwave broccoli until warm but not fully cooked.
5. Cover bottom of buttered lasagna sized pan with broccoli placing meat over broccoli layer.
6. Lightly cook carrots until tender and place over meat layer.
7. Lightly cook carrots until tender and place over meat layer.
8. Grate cheese over top and cover cheese with bread crumbs.
9. Mix sauce of light cream or milk with mayonnaise, basil and lemon juice and warm.
10. Pour sauce over all and add milk until at least 1/4 inch depth liquid.
11. Bake at 350 degrees for 45 minutes or until sauce is bubbling.
12. Be careful not to burn cheese and bread crumb topping.

Black Forest Smoked Squirrel

Ingredients:

Squirrels, cut into pieces
1 cup water
1 cup red wine
1/4 cup salt
4 tbsp. sugar
1/4 tsp. pepper
1 tsp. minced garlic
1 tbsp. monosodium glutamate

Directions:

1. Marinate squirrel pieces in mixture of rest of above ingredients for 12 to 16 hours in non-metal container.
2. If the squirrels are not covered, mix up more brine.
3. After marinating, drain squirrel pieces on paper toweling.
4. Place on cookie sheet to air dry for 1 to 2 hours.
5. Place pieces on oiled racks in electric smoker for 2 hours (2 pans of sawdust). Finish the squirrel in 225 degree oven, basting twice with butter for 2 hours.
6. Serve with crackers.

Squirrel And Gravy

Ingredients:

6 squirrels
1 slice bacon
1 cup all-purpose flour
1 can condensed milk

Directions:

1. Cut up 6 squirrels and put in large pot to boil.
2. Slice of bacon can be added for flavor.
3. Cook gently until meat is done.
4. Use enough water to cover meat plus several inches over.
5. Remove from water when done. Can be floured and fried lightly.
6. Bring liquid to boil.
7. Beat flour into condensed milk until smooth.
8. Gradually add to liquid.
9. Add salt and pepper to taste. Serve with buttermilk biscuits.

Fruited Squirrel

Ingredients:

2 squirrels, cut in serving pieces
12 prunes
1/4 cup raisins
3 tbsp. vinegar
6 gingersnaps, crumbled
1/2 tsp. salt
Pinch of mixed whole pickling spices
1 med. onion, fine diced
3 tbsp. brown sugar
1 tbsp. butter
2 tbsp. flour, browned

Directions:

1. Cook squirrel in salted water to cover until tender.
2. Remove meat.
3. To liquid add all ingredients except flour, simmer a few minutes.
4. Thicken with flour dissolved in 1/4 cup cold water.
5. Add meat, heat thoroughly.

Cajun Squirrel Stew

Ingredients:

4 squirrels, cut into pieces
1 cup chopped onion
4 cloves garlic
1/2 cup burgundy wine
1 tbsp. chopped parsley
1 tbsp. flour
1 stick butter
1/2 cup chopped green bell pepper
1 tbsp. Worcestershire sauce
1 tbsp. chopped onion tops
4 oz. or more mushrooms
Creole seasoning

Directions:

1. Cut each squirrel into 8 pieces.
2. Season with creole seasoning.
3. Melt butter in a Dutch oven and fry squirrel pieces until browned all over (and starts to stick to the pot).
4. Add a cup of chopped onions, 1/2 cup of bell peppers and 4 cloves of garlic. When vegetables are soft, add a small amount of cold water and Worcestershire sauce.
5. Cover pot and let simmer one hour.
6. Stir well, add 1/2 cup wine.
7. Cook until tender.
8. Add flour to mushroom liquid, onion tops, parsley and mushrooms.
9. Cook 5 minutes.
10. Combine with squirrels. Serve over rice.

Paprika Squirrel Stew and Greens

Ingredients:

3 squirrels, cut into serving pieces
Salt
Flour for dusting
1/3 cup olive oil
2 cups sliced onion
3 garlic cloves, minced
1 heaping tbsp. tomato paste
1 cup white wine
1/4 cup cider vinegar
1 heaping tsp. dried savory or oregano
1/2 tsp. red pepper flakes
1 heaping tbsp. paprika
2 to 3 cups of whole peeled tomatoes, torn into large pieces
1 pound smoked sausage, such as kielbasa or linguica, sliced
into bite-sized pieces
1 pound greens, kale, chard, collards, wild greens, etc
black pepper to taste

Directions:

1. Salt the squirrel pieces well and then dust in flour. Heat the
   olive oil in a large Dutch oven or other heavy, lidded pot over
   medium-high heat. Brown the squirrels in batches, being sure to
   not overcrowd the pot. Move the browned pieces to a plate or
   cutting board while you cook the rest.
2. When the squirrels have been nicely browned, remove them all
   from the pot and add the onion. Saute the onion until it just
   begins to brown on the edges, about 6 to 8 minutes.
3. Add the garlic and cook another minute.
4. Add the tomato paste, mix well and cook this for 2 to 3 minutes,
   stirring often.
5. Pour in the white wine, vinegar and about 1 quart of water.
6. Add the savory, red pepper flakes and paprika, then the torn-up
   tomatoes, then the squirrel.
7. Mix well and bring to a simmer.

8. Add salt to taste and cook gently until the squirrel wants to fall off the bone, about 90 minutes. Fish out all the squirrel pieces and pull them off the bone -- this makes the stew a lot easier to eat. Return them to the pot.
9. Add the smoked sausage and the greens and cook until the greens are done, about 10 minutes (If you are using collards, they need more than 10 minutes to cook so adjust accordingly).
10. Add salt, black pepper, chile and vinegar to taste and serve with crusty bread.

Honey-Cider Squirrel

Ingredients:

2 young squirrels, dressed whole and halved
2 crushed bay leaves
1/2 cup thick honey
1 pt. apple cider
1 tbsp. cornstarch, mixed with 2 tbsp. water

Directions:

1. Wipe squirrel halves dry and lay on broil rack. Coat completely with honey. Broil about 6 inches from heat for 8 minutes. Turn, coat again with honey, and broil 8 minutes more. Transfer to large, shallow baking dish or bottom of roaster.
2. Pour in the cider and add bay leaves.
3. Place in preheated 350 degree oven and roast for 1 hour or until meat is well down. Transfer to serving platter and keep warm. Strain pan juices into saucepan over medium heat thicken with the cornstarch mixture. Serve on side.

South Georgia Squirrel Stew

Ingredients:

1 gallon cold water
2 squirrels
2 tsp. salt
1/2 tsp. pepper
2 lg. onions, sliced
2 cup fresh okra, sliced
3 cup tomatoes, peeled
2 cup fresh lima beans
2 cup fresh carrots
5 potatoes, diced
4 cup fresh corn

Directions:

1. Bring water to a boil. Slowly add pieces of squirrel with bone left in. Be very careful not to boil rapidly at any time.
2. Add salt and pepper.
3. Add onions, okra, lima beans, tomatoes, carrots, and potatoes.
4. Add water occasionally and cook slowly for 4 hours. Then add corn and cook for 1 hour. Lower heat and stir occasionally to prevent scorching.
5. Add 3 oz. of butter just before serving.

Ozark Squirrel With Mushrooms

Ingredients:

1 squirrel, cleaned, dressed and disjointed
1/3 cup flour
1 tsp. salt
1/4 tsp. pepper
6 strips bacon, diced
1 clove garlic, minced
1 tsp. thyme
1 tbsp. tomato paste
2 cup chicken broth
1 cup mushrooms, sauteed in butter

Directions:

1. Dredge squirrel in seasoned flour.
2. Cook diced bacon over moderate heat and remove browned bits. Saute squirrel in bacon fat until browned on both sides.
3. Add garlic, thyme, tomato and chicken broth.
4. Cover and simmer about 1 hour or until tender. Serve with sauteed mushrooms, grits and green salad.

Roast Squirrels

Ingredients:

3 sm. squirrels
1/4 cup lemon juice
1/2 cup milk or cream
1/2 tsp. salt
1/2 tsp. onion juice
3/4 cup cooking oil
2 cup bread crumbs
1 cup sliced mushrooms, sauteed
1/8 tsp. pepper
4 tbsp. olive oil or bacon fat

Directions:

1. Dress and clean squirrels, wash in several waters and dry.
2. Cover with cooking oil mixed with lemon juice and let stand for 1 hour.
3. Combine crumbs, with just enough milk to moisten, mushrooms, salt, pepper and onion juice. Stuff squirrels with this mixture, sew and truss.
4. Place in roaster. Brush with olive oil or bacon fat. Roast uncovered in slow oven (325 degrees) until tender, 1 1/2 to 1 3/4 hours. Baste every 15 minutes with fat. Serve with gravy.

Squirrel Gumbo

Ingredients:

7 tbsp. flour
3 tbsp. corn oil
4-5 sm. squirrels
3 qt. cold tap water
1 whole onion, chopped
1/4 cup chopped green onion tops
Salt to taste
1 lb. smoked sausage, cut into bite size pieces
1/4 cup chopped parsley
Red pepper to taste

Directions:

1. Put oil in pan and heat until warm.
2. Stir in flour and cook, stirring constantly, over medium heat until mixture is brown. Scrape bottom often to keep roux from burning; set aside. Put roux in deep gumbo pot.
3. Add water. Set on medium heat and stir until blended.
4. Add chopped onion, squirrel, salt and red pepper.
5. Cook for 1/2 hour, then add sausage.
6. Cook for 1 hour or until meat is tender.
7. Add onion tops and parsley; cook for 15 minutes more.

Greek Squirrel

Ingredients:

1/4 cup olive oil
1 (3 pound) Squirrel, cut into pieces
2 bay leaves
1 tsp. salt
4 whole allspice berries
1/2 tsp. oregano
1 lemon, juiced
1/2 cup white wine
Wrm water, to cover

Directions:

1. Heat 1/4 cup olive oil in a large saucepan over medium heat. Fry Squirrel pieces in hot oil until evenly browned.
2. Season with bay leaves, salt, allspice berries, oregano, and lemon juice to the saucepan.
3. Pour white wine over the Squirrel.
4. Bring the mixture to a simmer.
5. Cook 4 to 5 minutes.
6. Add enough water to the saucepan to cover squirrel completely.
7. Bring the liquid to a simmer; cook until Squirrel is cooked through and the water is evaporated, about 40 minutes.

Squirrel Fricassee

Ingredients:

2 squirrels, dressed
1 1/2 tsp. salt
1/2 cup flour
1 tsp. grated onion
1/2 cup shortening
1/2 cup water
1 1/2 cup milk
Pepper to taste

Directions:

1. Cut squirrel in 6 pieces.
2. Combine salt, pepper and flour, roll squirrel in mixture. Heat shortening in iron skillet and brown pieces slowly on all sides, about 15 minutes.
3. Add 1/4 cup of water, reduce heat and simmer until tender, about 30 minutes.
4. Add remaining water as needed.

Squirrel Jambalaya

Ingredients:

1 med. squirrel
Salt
Red pepper
3 tbsp. cooking oil
2 lg. onions, chopped
3 stalks celery, chopped
1 clove garlic, chopped (optional)
1/4 green pepper, chopped
4 tbsp. chopped parsley
2 cup uncooked rice, washed
1 1/2 cup water
2 tsp. salt

Directions:

1. Cut squirrel into serving pieces; season well with salt and red pepper. Saute squirrel in oil until brown; remove from skillet. Saute onions, celery, garlic, green pepper and parsley in oil until wilted. Put squirrel back into skillet; cover.
2. Cook slowly about 30 minutes or until squirrel is tender.
3. Add rice and water.
4. Stir thoroughly 2-3 minutes.
5. Add salt; cook slowly about 30 minutes or until rice is cooked.

Squirrel Pot Pie

Ingredients:

3 grey or fox squirrels
3 tbsp. butter
1 tsp. salt
Rounds of biscuit crust
1/2 cup flour
1 chopped onion
1/4 tsp. pepper

Directions:

1. Skin, dress, and clean squirrel. Disjoint.
2. Roll in flour.
3. Melt 2 tbsps. butter in saucepan. Saute squirrel until brown.
4. Add 1 quart boiling water, onion, salt and pepper.
5. Cover closely and simmer 1 hour. Lay rounds of crust on squirrel.
6. Cover. Boil 15 minutes.
7. Remove crust and squirrel to hot platter. Blend 1 tbsp. flour and 1 tbsp. melted butter and add to liquid, mixing well.
8. Pour over squirrel and crust. If desired lemon juice, sherry or Worcestershire sauce may be added to gravy before serving.

Crockpot Squirrel

Ingredients:

3 to 5 squirrel, cut into halves
1/4 cup brown sugar, firmly packed
1/4 cup soy sauce
3 tbsp. lemon or lime juice
1/4 cup water
1/4 tsp. garlic powder
1/4 tsp. ground ginger

Directions:

1. Place squirrel halves in crockpot.
2. Mix all other ingredients in a bowl and pour over meat.
3. Cover and cook on low heat for 6 to 8 hours. Thicken gravy with flour mixed with water.

Rabbit Stew with Coconut Cream

Ingredients:

/4 cup oil for frying
1 (2 pound) squirrel, cleaned and cut into pieces
1 large onion, chopped
2 cloves garlic, chopped
1 green bell pepper, seeded and sliced into strips
1 red bell pepper, seeded and sliced into strips
1 bird's eye chile, seeded and minced
1 large tomatoes - peeled, seeded and chopped
1 3/4 cups chicken stock
1 tsp. salt
1 tsp. ground black pepper
2/3 cup cream of coconut

Directions:

1. Heat the oil in a skillet over medium-high heat. Fry the squirrel pieces until browned on the outside. Transfer to a soup pot or large saucepan.
2. Add the onion, garlic, green pepper, red pepper and chile pepper to the skillet; cook and stir until onion is transparent. Transfer to the saucepan.
3. Add the tomatoes, chicken stock, salt and pepper to the saucepan, and bring to a boil. Simmer over medium-low heat for about 2 hours.
4. Remove the squirrel pieces with a slotted spoon, and keep warm.
5. Turn the heat up to high under the saucepan, and boil the liquid until it has reduced by half.
6. Return the squirrel pieces to the pan, and stir in the coconut milk.
7. Cook, stirring gently, until heated through. Serve.

Squirrel With Rice And Potatoes

Ingredients:

2 old squirrels, cut up
1 green pepper, chopped
1 clove garlic, chopped
1 cup uncooked rice
1 onion, chopped
1/4 cup chopped celery
3 med. potatoes, chopped
Salt and pepper

Directions:

1. Brown squirrels in skillet with small amount of grease.
2. Pressure cook for 15 minutes to tenderize.
3. Saute onion, green pepper, celery, and garlic in skillet drippings; add rice, squirrel, potatoes, seasoning and enough liquid to cook rice and potatoes.
4. Cover; cook slowly until tender.

Steamed Squirrel

Ingredients:

1 squirrel
1/2 cup flour
Salt and pepper to taste
Meat tenderizer
Herb seasoning (opt.)
1 pod of dried red pepper, crushed
1/4 cup onion

Directions:

1. Dress and section squirrel. Soak in salt water until free of blood.
2. Roll in flour and fry in skillet with enough grease to bubble around each piece of meat. Over each section of squirrel, shake salt, pepper, meat tenderizer and herb seasoning.
3. Fry each side until tender and golden brown.
4. After each side is browned, turn heat down and add a glass of water to skillet.
5. Cover with a tight lid and steam until tender with dried red pepper and onion.

Squirrel With White Wine

Ingredients:

4 squirrels, cut in serving pieces
2 tbsp. butter
1/4 cup olive oil
Salt
Pepper
2 cloves garlic, crushed
1/2 tsp. rosemary
1 cup dry white wine
1 cup chicken broth
1 tbsp. chopped parsley
2 cup sliced mushrooms

Directions:

1. Saute squirrel in butter and oil until lightly browned; add salt and pepper to taste, garlic, rosemary, wine and broth; simmer until nearly done, turning often.
2. Add parsley and mushrooms, cook 5 minutes.

Beer Basted Rabbit

Ingredients:

3 pounds squirrel meat
2 tbsps. garlic salt
2 (12 fluid oz.) cans beer

Directions:

1. Preheat grill to medium high and lightly oil grate.
2. Place squirrel meat on heated grill and season with garlic salt.
3. Pour beer into a medium bowl. Let meat cook 15 minutes, then start basting with beer every 10 minutes until done, about 30 minutes.

Squirrel Sauce Piquant

Ingredients:

2 or 3 chopped bell peppers
2 or 3 lg. squirrels
2 lg. onions, chopped fine
2 or 3 lg. garlic cloves
1 cup onion blades
2 stems celery, chopped
1/2 tsp. parsley

Directions:

1. Season squirrel well with salt, pepper, red and black.
2. Heat 1/4 cup oil in iron pot, add squirrel and slowly simmer until all moisture is absorbed and meat is slightly brown.
3. Remove meat from pot and wash pot. Heat 3 or 4 tbsps. oil in clean pot, add vegetables and simmer slowly until all moisture is gone.
4. Do not brown.
5. Add 1 can tomato sauce, flour and water paste until slightly thick.
6. Add meat, bring to a boil and reduce heat to low.
7. Simmer slowly until meat is tender. Serve over hot cooked rice.

Squirrel Skillet Pie

Ingredients:

1 lg. squirrel
1/2 cup diced green peppers
1/4 cup flour
1/2 cup chopped onions
1/4 cup chopped celery
1/2 stick butter
1 tube homestyle biscuits
Salt and pepper

Directions:

1. Cut square into pieces.
2. Place in pan along with celery a pinch of salt and pepper and enough water to cover meat.
3. Place on burner and simmer until tender. Cool. Strip meat from bones, save broth.
4. Melt butter in iron frying pan, saute green peppers and onions. add flour and enough broth to make gravy.
5. Add meat, cook on low until gravy thickens.
6. Add biscuits to the top.
7. Place in oven at 425 degrees and bake for 8-10 minutes or until biscuits are golden brown.

Squirrel Cakes

Ingredients:

2 squirrels
1 sm. onion, minced
1 tsp. parsley flakes
1/2 cup crushed corn flakes
1 can golden mushroom soup, undiluted
Butter

Directions:

1. Parboil meat in salted water until tender, 20 to 30 minutes (longer for other meats).
2. Remove the meat from bones and cut into very fine pieces or grind.
3. Mix with onion, parsley, corn flakes. Moisten with enough soup to shape into small flat cakes. Fry in hot butter until well browned on both sides. Heat rest of soup. Serve cakes with a spoonful of soup over each helping.

Squirrel and Dumplings

Ingredients:

5-6 squirrels
4 cup water to cover meat
1 large onion, sliced
1 cup celery with leaves, chopped
1 medium carrot, scraped and sliced
2 tsp. salt
1/4 tsp. black pepper
1/2 cup cold water (for gravy)

Dumplings Ingredients:

2 cup sifted flour
3 tsp. baking powder
1 tsp. salt
2 tbsp. shortening
1/4 cup parsley, optional
1 cup water, approximately

Squirrel Directions:

1. Combine meat, water, vegetables, salt and black pepper in a large kettle with tight cover.
2. Cover, heat to a boil and simmer until meat is tender (about 1 to 1 & 1/2 hours).
3. Remove meat from broth and pick out bones.
4. Strain broth and mash vegetables through strainer into broth.
5. Add water to make 5 cups.
6. Return to heat and boil.
7. Stir 1/2 cup cold water into 6 Tbsps. flour to make gravy, stirring constantly until gravy thickens and boils (about 1 minute).
8. Season to taste.
9. Directions for Dumplings: Mix flour, baking powder and salt in a bowl.
10. Cut in shortening until crumbly, stir in parsley and enough water to moisten flour. Dough should be soft.

11. Drop dumpling batter into steaming kettle in 12 or more mounds.
12. Cover and cook for 20 minutes. Enjoy!

Squirrel Chowder

Ingredients:

2 squirrels
Chicken parts, as desired
1 lb. lean beef, cubed
1 cup celery, sliced
1 can corn
2 med. onions, sliced
Salt
Pepper
1 can tomato juice
1 can green beans
4 potatoes, cubed
3 carrots, sliced
1 can peas

Directions:

1. Combine meat, celery, corn, onions, salt, and pepper.
2. Cover with water.
3. Cook until meat is almost tender.
4. Add tomato juice, green beans, potatoes, carrots, and peas.
5. Cook until tender.
6. Remove bones and serve.

Applejack Squirrel

Ingredients:

3 squirrels (1 lb. each) cut in serving pieces
1 1/2 cup applejack (apple liqueur)
1 cup cream, warmed
2 tsp. instant flour
Salt
Pepper
Flour
1/4 cup diced bacon
2 tbsp. butter
1 tbsp. butter

Directions:

1. Wipe meat dry, then dust it with flour, salt, and pepper.
2. In a large skillet, fry bacon until it is golden, but do not brown.
3. Add meat and brown.
4. Pour in applejack, cover, and simmer until meat is tender and liquid almost evaporated.
5. Add butter and stir.
6. Remove meat to platter.
7. Add cream to pan.
8. Stir in remaining butter.
9. Sprinkle with instant flour. Continue to heat, stirring, until thickened.
10. Pour over meat.

Buttlemilk Batter Fried Squirrel

Ingredients:

1 1/2 cup flour
2 tsp. baking powder
Dash of salt
Enough buttermilk to make thick batter
1/4 tsp. pepper

Directions:

1. Soak squirrel overnight in salt water or with piece of charcoal. Parboil squirrel until tender, salt to taste.
2. Remove from liquid and drain on paper towel. Dip in batter and fry quickly in hot oil.

Squirrel Soup

Ingredients:

2 squirrels
6 cup water
3 tbsp. chicken bouillon
1 doz. peppercorns
1/4 tsp. thyme
1 tsp. salt
1 (10 oz.) can tomato soup
1 (16 oz.) can tomatoes, mashed
1/2 cup Bermuda onion, chopped
1/3 cup parsley flakes
1/2 cup butter
1 cup barley

Directions:

1. Cook first 6 ingredients together until meat is tender enough to pull off bone easily but not until it falls off.
2. Remove meat and strain broth.
3. Cut meat into small pieces.
4. Add to broth the tomato soup and mashed tomatoes with juice; add the onion, parsley flakes, and butter.
5. Bring to boil.
6. Add barley and simmer on low until tender.
7. Add meat and simmer 10 minutes.

Squirrel Confit

Ingredients:

2 grey squirrels, jointed into 6 pieces
150g of smoked streaky bacon, cut into lardons
1 banana shallot, sliced
1 celery stick, sliced
2 garlic cloves, finely chopped
1 bay leaf
2 sprigs of thyme
6 juniper berries
500ml of dry cider
salt
black pepper
sourdough bread
watercress
Olive oil

Directions:

1. Either use a crockpot or a casserole and your oven on a very low setting, approximately 120 degrees C. Start by layering the bacon down first, add the jointed squirrel and then scatter over the remaining vegetables, spices and herbs
2. Season generously and pour over the cider. Set the crock-pot to low, cover and then leave for 6-8 hours. The principle point here is to melt the bacon into submission and cook the squirrel meat until very, very tender
3. Leave to cool then pour the stock through a sieve, reserving the liquid.
4. Add the squirrel and as much of the bacon as possible to a bowl. Using your hands, pick the squirrel meat - this is a little bit fiddly and time consuming but you want to make sure that no tiny bones remain. Pick the meat over a metal bowl and listen out for any pings

5. When you have removed all the meat, combine with the bacon and mash together with a fork. Transfer to a food processor if you want a smoother pâté but I prefer it rough (no giggling at the back). If the mixture is a little bit dry, add a spoonful of leftover liquor but not too much
6. Spoon the mix into ramekins and put to one side. Take your block of unsalted butter and clarify by heating and melting in a saucepan on the hob, skimming any scum that rises to the top, whilst the chalky deposits fall to the bottom. The golden stuff in-between is what you are after
7. Carefully pour the clarified butter over the top of the squirrel, leaving just a thin layer, and place in the fridge to chill for an hour. Before serving, take the ramekins out of the fridge and bring to room temperature
8. When ready to serve, toast your sourdough and dress the watercress lightly in olive oil.
9. Arrange on a plate with the potted squirrel and a scattering of pickles

Squirrel Hand Pie

Dough Ingredients:

1/2 cup acorn flour
1 3/4 cups flour
1/2 tsp. baking powder
1 tsp. salt
3/4 cup whole milk
1/2 cup duck fat, lard, butter or shortening

Filling Ingredients:

3 tbsps. bacon fat
1 cup finely shredded cabbage
1 cup minced yellow or white onion
3/4 pound shredded and chopped squirrel meat
1 cup diced apple, peeled and cored
1/2 cup toasted, chopped black walnuts
1/2 tsp. Cavender's seasoning, or black pepper
1/2 cup warm stock, squirrel, chicken or something light
2 tsps. sorghum syrup or molasses
1 cup shredded gruyere, emmental or jarlsberg cheese (optional)

Dough Directions:

1. Mix the flours, baking powder and salt in a large bowl.
2. In a small pot, heat the milk until it's steaming, then turn off the heat.
3. Stir in the fat until it's mostly melted in; a few bits that aren't melted are fine.
4. Mix the wet ingredients into the dry with a fork until it's a shaggy mass. Knead this all together until you have a smooth ball, then shape it into a cylinder.
5. Wrap the dough in plastic wrap and set it in the fridge for at least 2 hours and up to overnight.

Filling Directions:

1. Heat the bacon fat in a large pan over medium-high heat and add the cabbage and onions. Saute until softened, about 6 to 8 minutes. Salt this as it cooks.
2. Add the squirrel meat, apple, walnuts and Cavender's seasoning (or black pepper), stir well and cook for a few minutes.
3. Stir the sorghum syrup in with the stock until combined, then pour this into the pan with everything else.
4. Stir this well and let it cook another few minutes so the ingredients absorb the liquid. Turn off the heat and let the filling cool.

Pies Directions:

1. If you have a tortilla press, get it out and cut a heavy plastic bag apart to make two plastic sheets that you'll use to keep the dough off the metal of the press. If you don't have a press, lay out a work space and flour it well.
2. Cut the dough into anywhere between 8 and 10 pieces, trying to keep them about the same size. Put half the pieces back in the fridge.
3. Roll a piece into a flat, disc and set it on a piece of plastic on the press. Put the other piece of plastic over it and squash the dough into a thin disc. I find that I do one squeeze, then adjust the dough so it's perfectly centered in the tortilla press.
4. If you don't have a press, roll the dough balls into flat discs about 1/8 of an inch thick.
5. Remove the dough from the plastic and put about 1/4 cup of filling on one side of the disc.
6. Sprinkle some shredded cheese on top if you'd like. Fold over the dough to make a half-moon and seal. Crimp the edges with a fork and set on a floured baking sheet.
7. Repeat with the rest of the dough.
8. Bake at 400F for 25 minutes. Move to a cooling rack for about 10 minutes before you eat them.

Squirrel Brunswick

Ingredients:

10 squirrels, disjointed
2 cans corn
1/2 lb. salt pork, diced
5 lb. potatoes, diced
2 qt. canned tomatoes
3 lb. onions, diced
2 lb. lima beans
1 cup diced celery
Salt and pepper to taste
1/4 cup Worcestershire sauce
Flour

Directions:

1. Place the squirrels in a large kettle with enough water to half cover and bring to a boil.
2. Cover the kettle. Simmer until squirrels are tender and cool.
3. Remove squirrels from stock and remove meat from bones.
4. Place squirrels back in stock and add remaining ingredients except flour.
5. Cook for 2 hours. Thicken with small amount of flour mixed with water and simmer for 30 minutes longer.

Squirrel Maison D'ete

Ingredients:

4 squirrels
Lemon juice
Salt and pepper to taste
Flour
1 pt. cream

Directions:

1. Cut the squirrels in serving pieces.
2. Sprinkle with lemon juice and place in a bowl. Refrigerate overnight. Wipe with a damp cloth and rub with salt and pepper.
3. Dredge with flour and fry in small amount of fat in a skillet for about 40 minutes or until brown.
4. Place in a casserole and add cream.
5. Bake at 425 degrees for 20 minutes.

Simple Tender Fried Squirrel

Ingredients:

2 squirrels skinned, gutted, and cut into pieces
1 bell pepper
1 onion

Directions:

1. Cut up squirrels, pepper and onion.
2. Put in a pan and bring to a boil.
3. Simmer for one hour.
4. Roll in flour.
5. Heat a small amount of oil in a skillet until hot.
6. Sprinkle lightly with garlic salt.
7. Brown on both sides slightly, and serve.

Curried Squirrel Puffs

Ingredients:

3-4 squirrels
1 large baking potato, cut into 1/2" cubes
1 cup of green peas
2 large carrots, cut as for the potato
Garlic (at least 2 cloves, more is better)
1/4 cup finely minced onion
1/2 tsp fresh ground ginger
Salt to taste
Ground pepper to taste
Curry powder to taste
Wonton Wrappers

Directions:

1. First, put the squirrels in a pressure cooker for about 15 minutes, and cook until the meat flakes from the bones but it isn't mushy. Reserve the liquor from this process.
2. Flake the meat off into a bowl, and mince coarsely.
3. To the squirrel meat, add the rest of the ingredients, except the curry powder.
4. Put enough of the pot liquor in to just come up to the top of the mixture (if you haven't got enough, add a little chicken broth).
5. Simmer uncovered until the vegetables are cooked and the liquid has evaporated.
6. You want a mixture that's stiff and not watery.
7. Add the curry powder salt, and pepper, and let sit at least a couple of hours to cool. Use circles or squares of pie crust dough or pre-cut won ton wrappers. If you're making these as a cocktail appetizer the final pieces should be bite-sized. 2-3" squares will give you triangular puffs, circles will make crescent-shaped ones.
8. Put a blob of filling (about 2 tsps., but the best amount will be obvious with practice) on the wrapper.
9. Wet the edges of the wrapper, fold over, and seal. The seal has to be tight or the stuff leaks out and makes a mess in the fry pot!

10. Deep fry the puffs in small batches in hot (350-375 degree) shortening.
11. Transfer to a piece of paper towel to drain.

Drunken Squirrel Nuggets

Ingredients:

2-3 squirrels (1 person) skinned, gutted, and cut into pieces
Flour
Cooking oil
Beer
Favorite seasonings
Lemon/orange Juice

Directions:

1. Remove all meat from squirrel bones (you may have to use a pressure cooker or something).
2. Cut it into little strips or cubes.
3. Make mixture of Lemon/Orange juice (or both) and a small amount of beer or wine. Soak strips/cubes in mixture over night.
4. Remove strips/cubes from mixture.
5. Put them in a bowl.
6. Add your favorite seasonings to bowl.
7. Shake together, then deep fry them.

Pink Squirrel Pie

Ingredients:

1/2 cup ground almonds
1 1/4 cup flour
1/2 tsp. salt
1/2 cup shortening
3-4 tbsp. milk
FILLING:
20 lg. marshmallows
1/2 cup milk
3 tbsp. white creme de cacao
3 tbsp. cream de nayaux
1 cup whipping cream, whipped

Directions:

1. Heat oven to 400 degrees.
2. In small bowl combine almonds, flour and salt.
3. Cut in shortening until particles are size of peas.
4. Add milk gradually, blend with fork to form dough.
5. Pat evenly in 8 or 9 inch pie pan, flute edges and prick bottom and sides with fork.
6. Bake for 10-12 minutes.
7. Cool.
8. In heavy saucepan, combine milk and marshmallows, cook over low heat, stirring constantly until marshmallows are melted.
9. Remove from heat, add liqueurs and cool completely.
10. Carefully fold in whipped cream.
11. Pour in pie shell and chill several hours.

Grilled Tequila Lime Squirrel

Ingredients:

2 squirrels, quartered

Marinade Ingredients:

1/2 cup tequila
1/2 cup lime juice (six to eight limes)
2 tbsps. olive oil
1 tsp. lime zest
2 tbsps. jarred jalapeno pepper slices
2 cloves garlic
2 tbsps. cilantro, chopped
1 tsp. cumin
1 tsp. salt
1/2 tsp. black pepper

Directions:

1. Mix marinade ingredients in a food processor.
2. Reserve ¼ cup to brush on squirrels as they grill.
3. Pour remaining marinade over squirrels in either a bowl or a one-gallon zip-style bag. Refrigerate overnight, flipping occasionally to cover well.
4. Grill the squirrel over a bed of charcoal or over medium heat on a gas grill for eight to 10 minutes per side, brushing often with reserved marinade. Top with diced chives.

Bamieh (Middle Eastern Okra Stew)

Ingredients:

2 tbsps. vegetable oil
2 large onions, chopped
Salt and ground black pepper to taste
2 pounds cubed lamb stew meat
3 tbsps. ground cinnamon
1 1/2 tsps. ground cumin
1 1/2 tsps. ground coriander
1 1/2 tbsps. garlic paste
5 (14.5 oz.) cans canned diced tomatoes, drained
1 1/2 tbsps. tomato paste
2 beef bouillon cubes
4 cups boiling water
2 pounds frozen sliced okra

Directions:

1. Heat the vegetable oil in a large pot over medium heat.
2. Stir in the onion, salt and black pepper.
3. Cook and stir until the onion has softened and turned a light golden brown, about 10 minutes.
4. Add the lamb, cinnamon, cumin, coriander, and garlic paste.
5. Cook on medium heat until the lamb starts to brown, 10 to 15 minutes, stirring occasionally.
6. Stir in the tomatoes and tomato paste; cook and stir for another 5 minutes.
7. Dissolve the beef bouillon cubes in 4 cups of boiling water.
8. Pour the broth into the pot with the lamb and stir in the okra. If necessary, add water to cover the okra.
9. Cover and simmer for 30 minutes, stirring occasionally.
10. Remove the cover and cook for another 45 minutes to 1 hour until the lamb is very tender and the stew reaches your desired thickness.

Hmong Squirrel Stew

Ingredients:

2 squirrels, cut into serving pieces
3 tbsps. vegetable oil
4 cloves garlic, minced
1 stalk of lemongrass, white part only, minced
3 to 5 red chiles, chopped
1 tbsp. minced galangal (optional)
2 tbsp. minced ginger, peeled
1 quart chicken stock
6 lime leaves or 1 tbsp. lime juice
1 tbsp. fish sauce or soy sauce
1 pound bok choy or chard, chopped
1/4 pound snow peas
1 tsp. ground Sichuan peppercorns (optional)
Salt

Garnish Ingredients:

1/2 cup chopped cilantro
1/2 cup chopped green onion
1/2 cup chopped mint

Directions:

1. Heat the vegetable oil in a large pot such as a Dutch oven.
2. Pat the squirrel pieces dry and brown them over medium-high heat in the oil.
3. Remove them as they brown and set aside.
4. Add the garlic, lemongrass, galangal, ginger and chiles and stir-fry over high heat for 90 seconds.
5. Return the squirrel to the pot and add the chicken stock, lime leaves and fish sauce. The broth should cover everything by about an inch.
6. If it does not, add some water.
7. Bring to a simmer and cook until the meat wants to fall off the bone, between 1 hour and 2 hours.
8. Remove the meat and shred it off the bones. Return it to the pot.

9. Add the bok choy and the snow peas and simmer until tender, about 10 minutes.
10. Add salt to taste and the ground Sichuan pepper.
11. Serve it in bowls over steamed rice.
12. Garnish with the cilantro, green onions and mint.

Cajun Squirrel Dirty Rice

Ingredients:

Meat from two squirrels
Hearts and livers from two squirrels
1.5 cups of long grain and wild rice blend
1 yellow onion, diced
1 bell pepper, diced
1 stalk celery, chopped
1 clove garlic, minced
4 cups chicken stock
2 cups water
2 tbsps. Cajun seasoning
1 tsp. ground thyme
2 bay leaves

Directions:

1. Cook the squirrel (not the hearts and livers) in either a slow cooker for 5-7 hours, or an Instant-Pot for 25 minutes. Allow to cool and strip the meat from the bones.
2. Dice the raw hearts and livers then set them aside. Give the pepper, onion and celery a rough chop.
3. In a large heavy pot over medium-high heat, saute the pepper, onion and celery for 7-10 minutes or until the onions are soft and cooked through.
4. Add the garlic and diced hearts and livers.
5. Cook another 3-5 minutes.
6. Add the rice, stock, boned-out squirrel meat, and water.
7. Add the Cajun seasoning and thyme.
8. Stir well.
9. Toss in the bay leaves.
10. Bring the mixture to a low boil, then reduce the heat and simmer, covered, for 25-30 minutes until the rice is done. Fluff with fork before serving.

About the Author

Laura Sommers is **The Recipe Lady!**

She is a loving wife and mother who lives on a small farm in Baltimore County, Maryland and has a passion for all things domestic especially when it comes to saving money. She has a profitable eBay business and is a couponing addict. Follow her tips and tricks to learn how to make delicious meals on a budget, save money or to learn the latest life hack!

Visit her Amazon Author Page to see her latest books:

amazon.com/author/laurasommers

Follow her on Pinterest:

Follow the Recipe Lady on **Pinterest**:

http://pinterest.com/therecipelady1

Visit the Recipe Lady's blog for even more great recipes:

http://the-recipe-lady.blogspot.com/

Other Books by Laura Sommers

Recipes for the Zombie Apocalypse, Cooking With
Shelf Stable Foods

Recipes for the Zombie Apocalypse II, Cooking With
Foraged Foods

Dandelion Recipes

Recipes for The Lumbersexual

Printed in Great Britain
by Amazon